AMAZING ANIMAL DISCOVERIES

by Ben Hubbard

Illustrated by Dragan Kordic

Contents

OXFORD

UNIVERSITY PRESS

Discovering Animals

Do you know how many types of animals there are in the world? There are over eight *million* species!

What is a species?

A species is a group of animals that are similar enough to each other that they can have offspring. For example, lions and tigers are both big cats but they are different species. Every species is given a special name in Latin – so lions are called *Panthera leo* and tigers are called *Panthera tigris*.

Did you know that we are still discovering animals? Scientists discover dozens of new species every year. To discover a new species, scientists must prove that no one else has found it first. They must then describe exactly what the species is like.

Some recently discovered animals are alive today, but others have been **extinct** for millions of years.

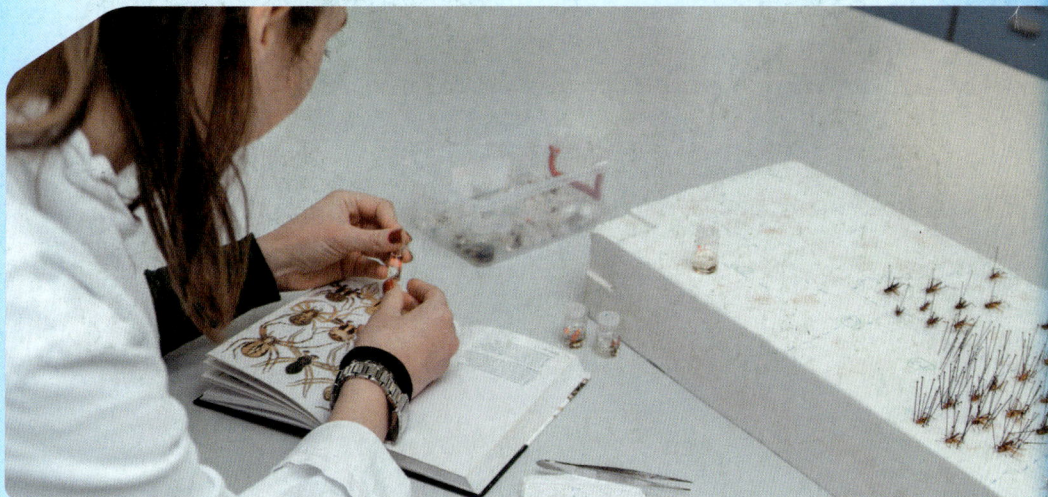

Scientists say we are <u>bound</u> to continue finding more animal species, because there are still so many places on Earth to explore. This book is all about the most amazing recent animal discoveries.

If we are <u>bound</u> to discover more animal species, is it definite that this will happen or is it unlikely to happen?

Seahorse Spotting

Do you have good <u>vision</u>? You'll need it to see this species of **pygmy** seahorse.

All pygmy seahorses are tiny – usually less than 20 millimetres long! However, it is not just their size that keeps them safe from hungry **predators**.

Pygmy seahorses' colouring gives them great **camouflage**.

You need good <u>vision</u> to see something tiny like this seahorse. Can you think of any other animals that you might need good <u>vision</u> to see?

There are seven species of pygmy seahorse in the world. This particular one was discovered in the sea near Japan. The bony ridge on its back makes it different from the other species.

bony ridge

tail

snout

Species: Japan pig
(Hippocampus japapigu)

Size: around 15 millimetres

Diet: plankton

Year species named: 2018

Finding Vipers

A new snake species has been discovered in India. It is called the Arunachal (*say* Ah-ruh-naht-shal) pit viper.

The Arunachal pit viper is a clever hunter. It has holes in its head that can detect heat from other creatures. This helps the viper <u>seek</u> its **prey** - even in the dark!

The viper can <u>seek</u> its prey in the dark. How would you <u>seek</u> something in the dark?

Vipers kill their prey by biting them. They have long fangs that inject powerful poison into an animal's flesh. These fangs are usually folded away, and only <u>emerge</u> when the viper opens its mouth. Then they spring forward, ready to bite.

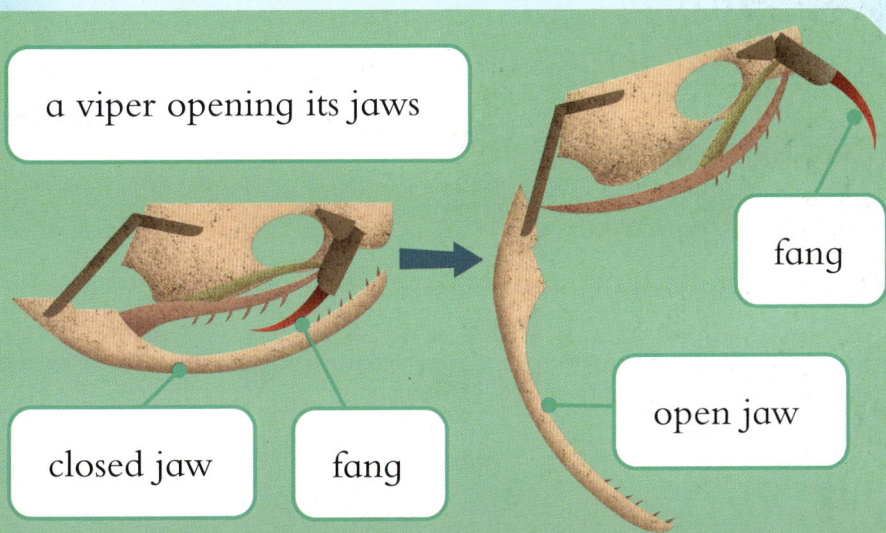

a viper opening its jaws

fang

open jaw

closed jaw

fang

Species: Arunachal pit viper
(*Trimeresurus arunachalensis*)

Diet: pit vipers eat birds, lizards, rodents

Year species named: 2018

The viper's fangs <u>emerge</u> when it opens its jaws. Does this mean its fangs go into its mouth or come out of its mouth?

Orangutans Calling

Orangutans are amazing animals and we're learning new things about them all the time. In 2017, a group of orangutans on the island of Sumatra were found to belong to a brand new species. The Tapanuli orangutan lives in the forest treetops.

Male orangutans talk to each other with long, loud calls.

flat cheeks

beard

orange hair

The Tapanuli orangutan is clever. It builds its bed from leaves and branches and stays up high, away from tigers that are a **threat**.

Unfortunately, the orangutan is also under threat from people who are cutting down its forests. There are only 800 Tapanuli orangutans left in the wild.

Species: Tapanuli orangutan *(Pongo tapanuliensis)*

Lives for: 40 years

Diet: pine cones, caterpillars, insects

Year species named: 2017

The Deepest Fish

A species of fish called the Swire's snailfish has been discovered living in the deepest part of the ocean: the Mariana Trench. The Trench is so deep that there is no light. There is also crushing pressure from the weight of the water. Few animals can survive there.

The Mariana Trench is about as deep as 33 Eiffel Towers stood on top of each other!

The deepest part of the Mariana Trench is over 10000 metres (10 kilometres) below sea level.

It is completely dark in the Trench, but shining a light from a submarine reveals that the Swire's snailfish is pink and as long as a pencil. Its skin is so delicate that you can see through it. The snailfish gulps down its prey using its unusual sucking mouth.

Species: Swire's snailfish
(*Pseudoliparis swirei*)
Length: 11 centimetres
Diet: shrimp, small crabs
Year species named: 2018

Underground Eels

Eels are long, thin fish that live in rivers and seas. However, swamp eels don't always live in water – instead, they can live in mud!

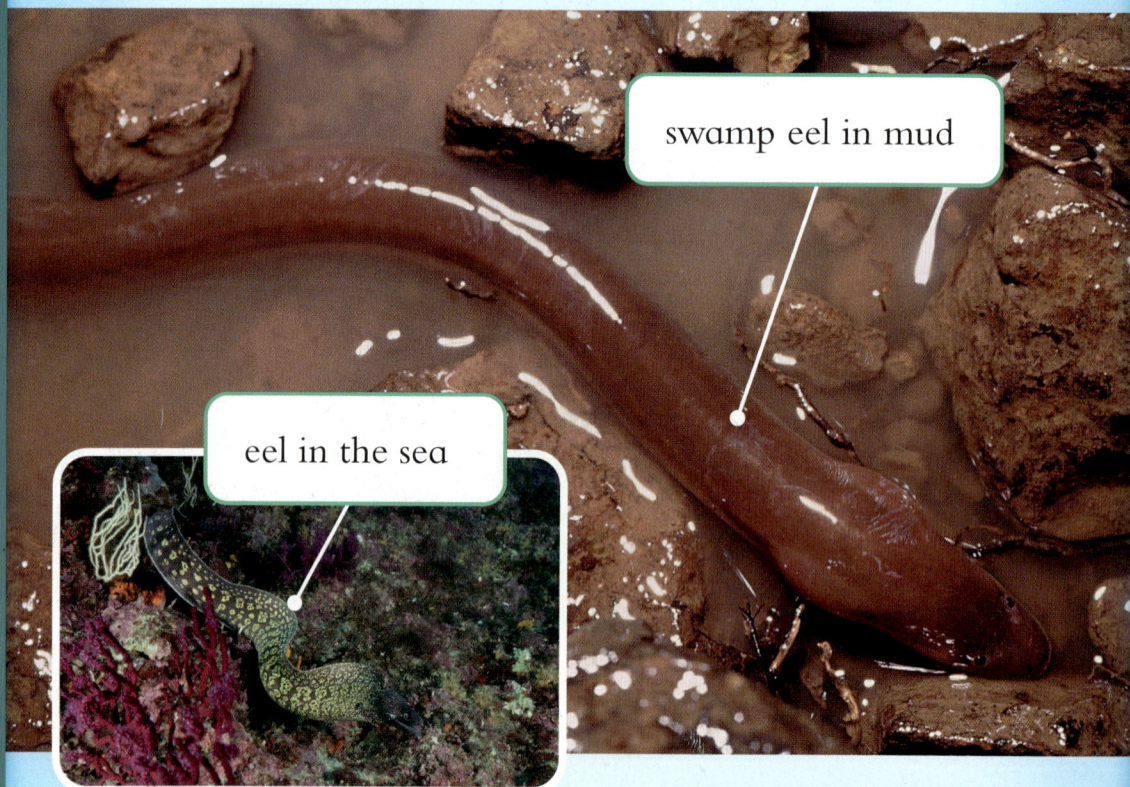

swamp eel in mud

eel in the sea

One newly discovered type of swamp eel was found underground in a rainforest, 50 metres from the nearest stream.

This new type of hypogean (*say* high-poa-jee-an) swamp eel **burrows** through the dark soil like a worm. Because there is no light underground, it doesn't need eyes and has no <u>vision</u>.

Most eels use **gills** to breathe underwater. However, this swamp eel does not have gills. Instead, it breathes through its mouth and its skin.

hypogean swamp eel

Species: hypogean swamp eel (*Monopterus rongsaw*)

Length: 18 centimetres

Diet: worms, tiny insects

Year species named: 2018

The swamp eel has no <u>vision</u>. Can you think of any other words the author could have used instead of '<u>vision</u>'?

Hopping Rats

Most rats have sharp teeth and eat almost anything, but not all rats are the same. Tweezer-beaked hopping rats have hardly any teeth. As for their food, earthworms are a <u>firm</u> favourite! They only live on the island of Luzon in the Philippines. Recently, two new species of this rat have been discovered.

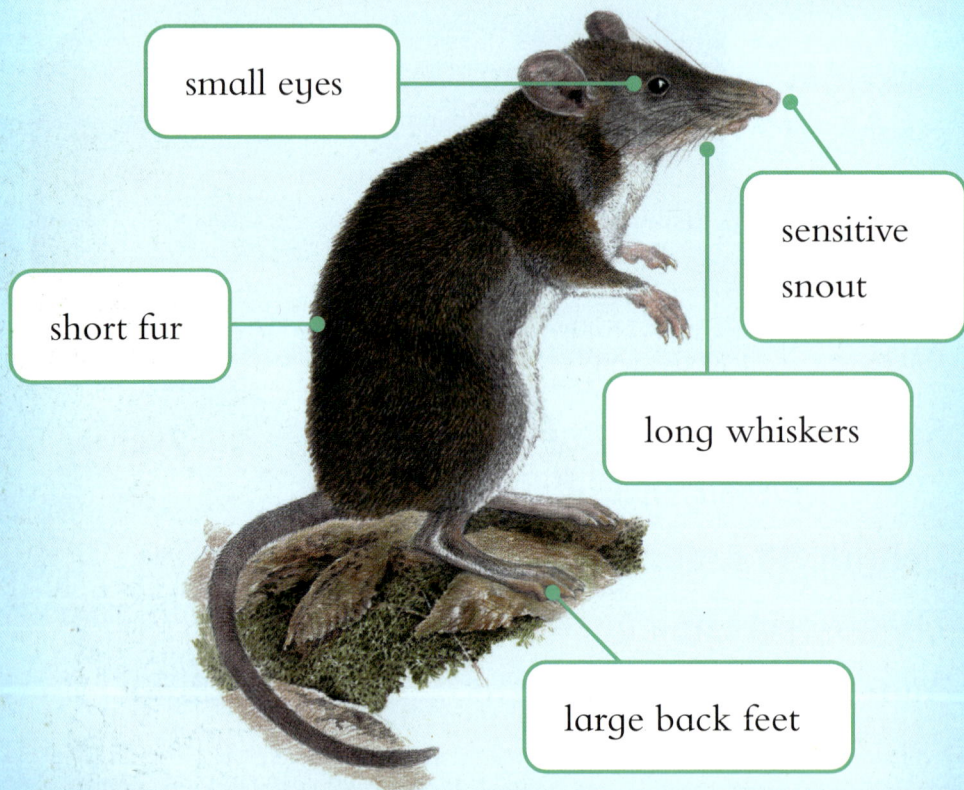

small eyes

sensitive snout

short fur

long whiskers

large back feet

Which meal is your <u>firm</u> favourite?

The tweezer-beaked hopping rat is rather strange. They can stand on their back legs and hop around like kangaroos! They make small paths in the forest and patrol these paths looking for earthworms, which they slurp up like strands of spaghetti.

Species: *Rhynchomys labo* and *Rhynchomys mingan*

Body length: 22 centimetres

Habitat: mountain forests

Year species named: 2019

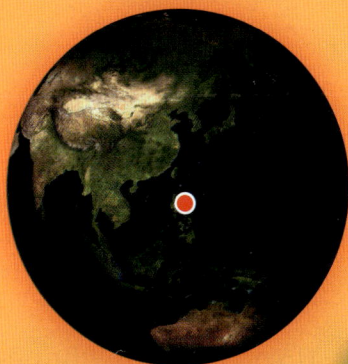

Beetle Disguise

Be <u>honest</u>, does this look like a beetle to you? The baffling beetle is hard to spot because it is attached to an ant!

The beetle is the exact size, shape and colour as an ant's abdomen (back part). The beetle attaches itself to an ant to travel around.

baffling beetle

If you are being <u>honest</u>, are you telling the truth or a lie?

The baffling beetle prefers army ants because they spend weeks marching to a place where there is more prey. The beetle grabs on to an ant with its mouth and stays attached to it until the ant stops – then it lets go. The ant and beetle then feed on prey in the new place. The beetle grabs on again before the ant leaves.

beetle's body

The beetle holds on using its powerful jaws.

beetle's jaws

ant's body

Species: baffling beetle
(*Nymphister kronaueri*)
Body length: 1.5 millimetres
Location: Costa Rica
Year species named: 2017

Cartoon-eyed Shark

Some sharks are massive, but others are very small. Dogfish are a type of small shark, and a new species of dogfish has emerged called the Genie's dogfish. It is small, skinny and stays near the bottom of the sea. It also has huge eyes. It looks more like a cartoon character than a fierce predator!

How big am I?

adult human (average height 1.65 metres)

great white shark (average length 3.8 metres)

Genie's dogfish (average length 60 centimetres)

The Genie's dogfish lives in the deep waters of the Atlantic Ocean. We do not know much about this species of dogfish, but we do know that it is under threat. Millions of dogfish are caught every year, and fishing boats are fishing deeper and deeper in the sea.

This fishing boat is catching sharks.

Species: Genie's dogfish
(Squalus clarkae)
Number of teeth: 50–53
Diet: squid, fish, crabs
Year species named: 2018

Wasp with a Saw

Wasps often sting if they feel threatened, but what if a wasp had a saw instead of a stinger? That is what scientists discovered on a species of wasp called *Dendrocerus scutellaris* (*say* Den-droa-se-rus skoo-tel-ar-is).

The wasp has a saw on its back.

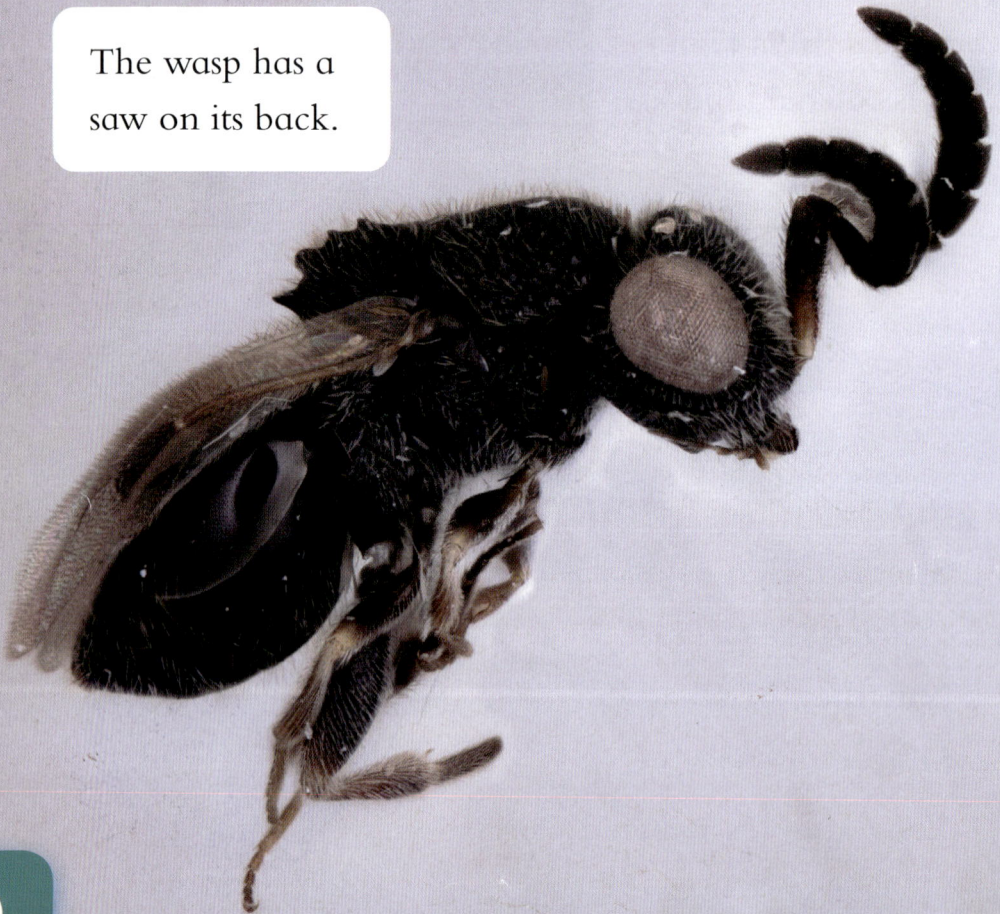

Scientists think this strange wasp is born inside the body of another creature! The mother wasp lays its eggs in insects and spiders. Baby wasps hatch from the eggs and cut their way out with their back saws. They then fly away to find another animal to lay their eggs inside.

If they sound scary, don't worry – the wasps are only the size of a tiny sesame seed.

Name: *Dendrocerus scutellaris*
Length: 2.7 millimetres
Location: Costa Rica
Year species named: 2018

Madagascar Minis

On the island of Madagascar, five new tiny frog species have been discovered. The frogs are so small that one could sit on your fingertip. They belong to a group known as 'narrow-mouthed frogs'.

The new frogs are the same length as a grain of rice.

Narrow-mouthed frogs live among the leaves on the forest floor. Being so small means they are very hard to find, and scientists have to study them through a **microscope**.

How big am I?

One of the narrow-mouthed frogs is the smallest frog ever found.

largest frog in the world (32 centimetres long)

smallest frog in the world (7.7 millimetres long)

The newly discovered frogs are in danger of becoming extinct because their forests are being cut down.

Dinosaur Remains

Sometimes we discover a new animal that is no longer alive. The animal has become extinct. So how can it be a new discovery? It is new to us because we did not know it existed. However, the animal left its remains behind. Finding these remains is very exciting!

Finding fossils

The dinosaurs died out around 66 million years ago. Sometimes their remains can be seen in fossils, which are bones that have turned to stone or the shapes of bones left in rock.

A new species of dinosaur called *Lingwulong shenqi* (say Ling-woo-long shen-chee) was recently discovered in China. It is a type of dinosaur called a sauropod. Sauropods were massive four-legged dinosaurs with long necks. They <u>required</u> long necks to eat the leaves from tall trees.

Name: *Lingwulong shenqi*

Length: over 15 metres

Diet: leaves, branches, plants

Fossil date: 174 million years ago

Year species named: 2018

This dinosaur <u>required</u> a long neck to eat leaves from tall trees. What would you <u>require</u> to reach something high up?

Dinosaur or Bird?

A very different dinosaur species that has been recently discovered was small, lived in trees and could fly. It had wings made from skin like a bat, and feathers too. That's why it is called *Ambopteryx* (*say* Am-bo-ter-ix) which means 'both wings'.

Species: *Ambopteryx longibrachium*

Diet: small animals, insects, plants

Fossil date: 163 million years ago

Year species named: 2017

Scientists learned about Ambopteryx from a fossilized skeleton. They think that Ambopteryx used its wings to glide from branch to branch and swoop in on its prey.

the *Ambopteryx* dinosaur fossil

How big am I?

*Ambopteryx (*average length 32 centimetres)

Diplodocus (average length 27 metres)

Tyrannosaurus rex (average length 12 metres)

adult human (average height 1.65 metres)

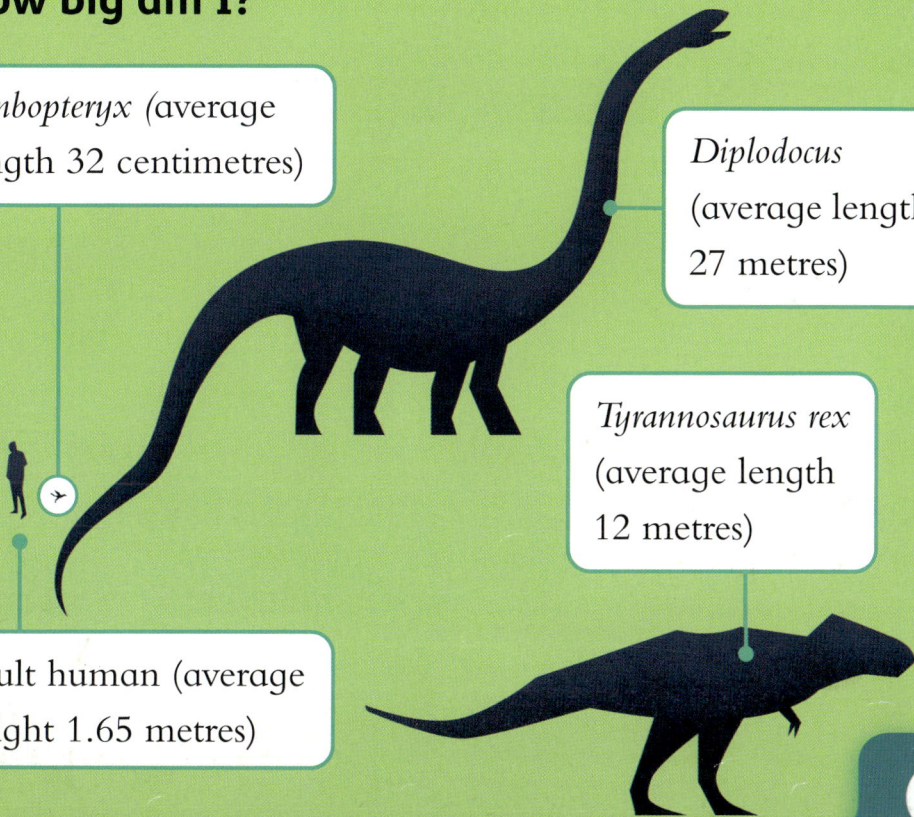

Ancient Lion

Not all ancient animals were dinosaurs. Some were more like the animals we see today. One such species just discovered was the **marsupial** lion called *Wakaleo schouteni* (*say* Wai-ka-lee-oh skoo-ten-ee). It lived in Australia around 25 million years ago.

fangs

The marsupial lion had two front fangs for slicing through flesh. It had a small body with strong shoulders and sturdy back legs. It might have been able to stand on its back legs like a cat can. Its strength also helped it climb trees, where it hunted for its prey.

Species: *Wakaleo schouteni*

Diet: lizards, frogs, birds and small mammals

Lived: 25 million years ago

Year species named: 2017

Scientists discovered the skull and leg bones of the lion. This told them information about the lion and where it lived.

Extinction Threat

Scientists say there are millions of animal species left to discover. Some may be alive today. Others will already be extinct.

Sometimes animals are made extinct by a massive event. Many scientists believe the dinosaurs died out when an **asteroid** struck the Earth, millions of years ago. The asteroid caused dust clouds which blocked out sunlight, and most animal life did not survive.

Climate change is a massive event threatening animals today. Climate change is warming the Earth and destroying habitats. It will make many animals extinct. Humans can slow down climate change by making changes to our lives, but it is a big task. It requires us to recycle, stop burning **fossil fuels** and prevent forests being cut down.

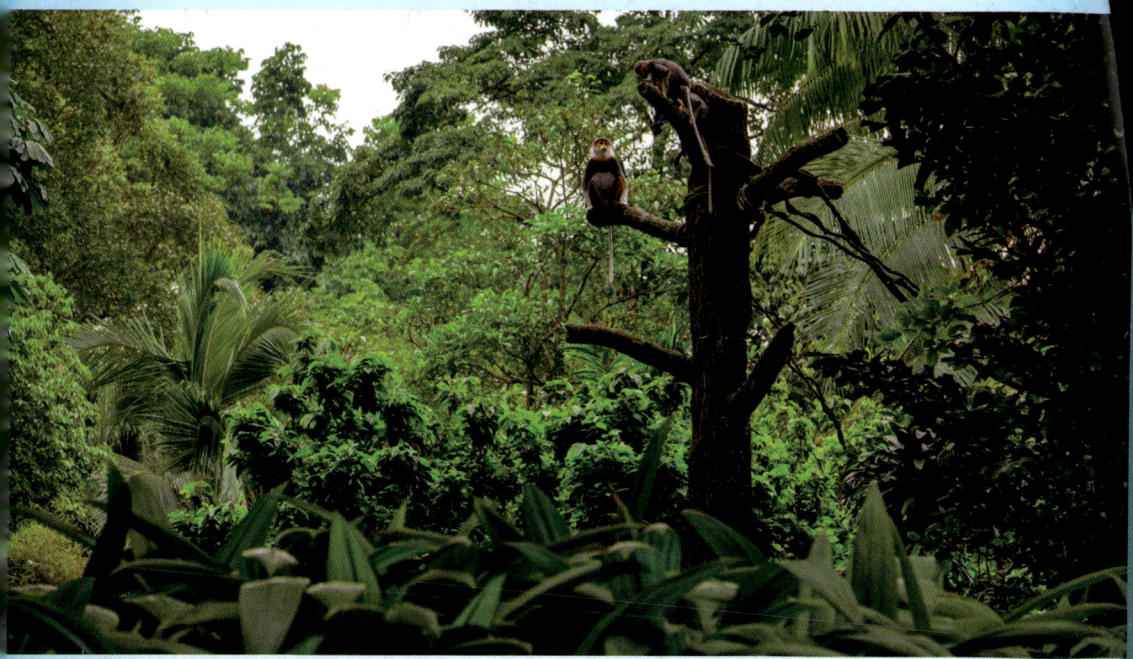

If we look after their homes, there will be many more amazing animals to discover in the future.

Why might slowing down climate change be a big task? What could you do to help?

~ary

d: a rocky object that travels around the Sun

~s: digs a tunnel in the ground

>uflage: using colours or shapes to blend into the rroundings

~nct: when a whole species has died out

;sil fuels: fuels like coal, gas or petrol

ills: the parts of the body that fish and eels use to breathe

marsupial: a type of animal that carries its babies in a pouch on its body

microscope: an instrument that makes very small things look bigger so you can see them

plankton: very tiny plants and animals that float in the sea

predators: animals that hunt other animals to eat

prey: an animal that is hunted by another animal for food

pygmy: a name used for some very small animals or plants

threat: danger

Index